MR. GANDHI AND THE EMANCIPATION OF THE UNTOUCHABLES

MAVEN BOOKS

MR. GANDHI AND THE EMANCIPATION OF THE UNTOUCHABLES

DR. B.R. AMBEDKAR

MAVEN BOOKS

Chennai   Trichy   Tirunelveli   New Delhi

An Imprint of **MJP Publishers**

ISBN 978-93-88191-89-0 **Maven Books**

All rights reserved   No. 44, Nallathambi Street,
Printed and bound in India   Triplicane, Chennai 600 005

MJP 727   © Publishers, 2018

Publisher :   **C. Janarthanan**

Publisher's Note

The legacy of a country is in its varied cultural heritage, historical literature, developments in the field of economy and science. The top nations in the world are competing in the field of science, economy and literature. This vast legacy has to be conserved and documented so that it can be bestowed to the future generation. The knowledge of this legacy is slowly getting perished in the present generation due to lack of documentation.

Keeping this in mind, the concern with retrospective acquiring of rare books has been accented recently by the burgeoning reprint industry. Maven Books is gratified to retrieve the rare collections with a view to bring back those books that were landmarks in their time.

In this effort, a series of rare books would be republished under the banner, "Maven Books". The books in the reprint series have been carefully selected for their contemporary usefulness as well as their historical importance within the intellectual. We reconstruct the book with slight enhancements made for better presentation, without affecting the contents of the original edition.

Most of the works selected for republishing covers a huge range of subjects, from history to anthropology. We believe this reprint edition will be a service to the numerous researchers and practitioners active in this fascinating field. We allow readers to experience the wonder of peering into a scholarly work of the highest order and seminal significance.

Maven Books

Contents

CHAPTER I

Total Population of the Untouchables

THE Decennial Census in India was at one time a very simple and innocent operation which interested only the Malthusians. None else took interest in it. Today the Census is a matter of a first rate concern to everybody. Not only the professional politician but the general public in India regards it as a matter of very grave concern. This is so because Politics in India has become a matter of numbers. It is numbers which give political advantage, to one community over another which does not happen anywhere else in the world. The result is that the Census in India is deliberately cooked for securing political advantages which numbers give. In this cooking of the Census the Hindus, the Muslims and the Sikhs have played their part as the chief chefs of the kitchen. The Untouchables and the Christians, who are also interested in their numbers, have no hand in the cooking of the Census, for the simple reason that they have no place in the administrative services of the country which deal with the operations of the Census. On the other hand the Untouchables are the people who are quartered, cooked and served by the Hindus, Muslims and the Sikhs at every Decennial Census. This has happened particularly in the last Census of 1940. The Untouchables of certain parts of the Punjab were subjected to systematic tyranny and oppression by the Sikhs. The object was to compel them to declare in the Census returns that they are Sikhs even though they are not. This reduced the number of the Untouchables and swelled the number of the Sikhs. The Hindus on their part carried on a campaign that nobody should declare his or her caste in the Census return. A particular appeal was made to the Untouchables. It was suggested to them that it is the name of the Caste that proclaims to the world that they are Untouchables and if they did not declare their caste name but merely said that they were Hindus, they would be treated just like other Hindus and nobody would know that they were really Untouchables. The Untouchables fell a victim to this stratagem and decided not to declare themselves as Untouchables in the Census return but to call themselves merely as Hindus. The result was obvious. It reduced the number of Untouchables and swelled the ranks of the Hindus. To what extent the cooking of the Census has taken place it is difficult to say. But there can be no doubt that the degree to which cooking was resorted to was considerable. The Census has been cooked all over. But it is the Untouchables who have suffered most from the cooking of the Census. That being so, the Census figure regarding the total population of the Untouchables in British India cannot be accepted as giving a correct total. But one cannot be far wrong if it was said that the present number of the Untouchables to British India is round about 60 million people.

CHAPTER II

The Importance of the Untouchables

MOST parts of the world have had their type of what Ward calls the lowly. The Romans had their slaves, the Spartans their helots, the British their villeins, the Americans their Negroes and the Germans their Jews. So the Hindus have their Untouchables. But none of these can be said to have been called upon to face a fate which is worse than the fate which pursues the Untouchables. Slavery, serfdom, villeinage have all vanished. But Untouchability still exists and bids fair to last as long as Hinduism will last. The Untouchable is worse off than a Jew. The sufferings of the Jew are of his own creation. Not so are the sufferings of the Untouchables. They are the result of a cold calculating Hinduism which is not less sure in its effect in producing misery than brute force is. The Jew is despised but is not denied opportunities to grow. The Untouchable is not merely despised but is denied all opportunities to rise. Yet nobody seems to take any notice of the Untouchables-some 60 millions of souls-much less espouse their cause.

If there is any cause of freedom in this Indian turmoil for independence it is the cause of the Untouchables. The cause of the Hindus and the cause of the Musalmans is not the cause of freedom. Theirs is a struggle for power as distinguished from freedom. Consequently it has always been a matter of surprise to me that no party and no organisation devoted to the cause of freedom has so far interested itself in the Untouchables. There is the American Weekly called "The Nation". There is the British Weekly called "Statesman". Both are powerful. Both are friends of India's freedom. I would mention the American

Labour and British Labour among organised bodies among the supporters of India's freedom. So far as I know none of these have ever championed the cause of the Untouchables. Indeed what they have done is what no lover of freedom would do. They have just identified themselves with the Hindu body calling itself the Indian National Congress. Now everybody in India, outside the Hindus, knows that whatever may be its title it is beyond question that the Congress is a body of middle class Hindus supplied by the Hindu Capitalists whose object is not to make Indians free but to be independent of British control and to occupy places of power now occupied by the British. If the kind of Freedom which the Congress wants was achieved there is no doubt that the Hindus would do to the Untouchables exactly what they have been doing in the past In the light of this apathy the Indian branch of the Institute of International Affairs may well be congratulated for having invited a paper for submission to the Institute of Pacific Relations, discussing the position of the Untouchables in India in the New Constitution. I must confess that this invitation for a statement on the position of the Untouchables under the new constitution came to me as an agreeable surprise and a great relief and it is because of this, that notwithstanding the many things with which lam preoccupied, I agreed to find time to prepare this paper.

CHAPTER III

The Political Demands of the Untouchables

The problem of the Untouchables is an enormous problem. As a matter of fact I have been for sometime engaged on a work dealing with this problem which will run into several hundred pages. All that I can do within the limits of this paper is to set out in a brief compass what the nature of the problem is and the solution which the Untouchables have themselves propounded. It seems to me that I cannot do better than begin by drawing attention to the following Resolutions which were passed at the All-India Scheduled Castes[1] Conference held in the city of Nagpur on the 18th and 19th July 1942 :-

RESOLUTION NO. II

CONSENT ESSENTIAL TO CONSTITUTION

"This Conference declares that no constitution will be acceptable to the Scheduled Castes unless,

    (i)   it has the consent of the Scheduled Castes,

    (ii)   it recognises the fact that the Scheduled Castes are distinct and separate from the Hindus and constitute an important element in the national life of India, and

    (iii)   contains within itself provisions which will give to the Scheduled Castes a real sense of security under the new constitution and which are set out in the following resolutions."

---

1. Under the Government of India Act of 1935 the Untouchables are designated as 'Scheduled Castes'.

RESOLUTION NO. III

ESSENTIAL PROVISIONS IN THE NEW CONSTITUTION

"For creating this sense of security in the Scheduled Castes: this Conference demands that the following provisions shall be made in the new Constitution:-

(1) That in the *budget* of every provincial Government an annual sum as may be determined upon by agreement be set apart for promoting the primary education among the children of the Scheduled Castes and another annual sum for promoting advanced education among them, and such sums shall be declared to be the first charge on the revenues of the Province.

(2) That provision shall be made by law for securing representation to the Scheduled Castes in all Executive Governments-Central and Provincial-the proportion of which shall be determined in accordance with their number, their needs and their importance.

(3) That provision shall be made by law for securing representation to the Scheduled Castes in the Public Services the proportion of which shall be fixed in accordance with their number, their needs and their importance. This Conference further insists that in the case of security services such as Judiciary, Police and Revenue, provision shall be made that the proportion fixed for the Scheduled Castes shall, subject to the rule of minimum qualification, be realised within a period of ten years.

(4) That provision shall be made by law for guaranteeing to the Scheduled Castes representation in all Legislatures and Local bodies in accordance with their number, needs and importance.

(5) That provision shall be made by law whereby the representation of the Scheduled Castes in

all Legislatures and Local Bodies shall be by the method of Separate Electorates.

(6) That provision shall be made by law for the representation of the Scheduled Castes on all Public Service Commissions, Central and Provincial."

RESOLUTION NO. LV.

SEPARATE SETTLEMENTS

"It is the considered opinion of this conference,

(a) that so long as the Scheduled Castes continue to live on the outskirts of the Hindu village, with no source of livelihood and in small number as compared to Hindus, they will continue to remain Untouchables and subject to the tyranny and oppression of the Hindus and will not be able to enjoy free and full life.

(b) That for the better protection of the Scheduled Castes from the tyranny and oppression of the Caste Hindus, which may take a worse form under Swaraj which cannot but be a Hindu Raj, and

(c) to enable the Scheduled Castes to develop to their fullest manhood, to give them economical and social security as also to pave the way for the removal of untouchability.

This Conference has after long and mature deliberation come to the conclusion that a radical change must be made in the village system now prevalent in India and which is the parent of all the ills from which the Scheduled Castes are suffering for so many centuries at the hands of the Hindus. Realising the necessity of these changes this conference holds that along with the Constitutional changes in the system of Government there must be a change in the village system now prevalent, made along the following lines:

(1) The constitution should provide for the transfer of the Scheduled Castes from their present habitation

and form separate Scheduled Caste villages away from and independent of Hindu village.

(2) For the settlement of the Scheduled Castes in new villages a provision shall be made by the constitution for the establishment of a Settlement Commission.

(3) All Government land which is cultivable and which is not occupied shall be handed over to the Commission to be held in trust for the purpose of making new settlements of the Scheduled Castes.

(4) The Commission shall be empowered to purchase new land under the Land Acquisition Act from private owners to complete the scheme of settlement of Scheduled Castes,

(5) The constitution shall provide that the Central Government shall grant to the settlement commission a minimum sum of Rupees five crores per annum to enable the Commission to carry out their duty to this behalf.

That it is unsound will be quite obvious to any One who will stop to examine the assumptions which are involved in the alleged efficacy and sufficiency of the territorial constituency. What are these assumptions ? To mention only those which are most important,

(1) It assumes that the majority of voters in a constituency represents the will of the constituency as a whole.

(2) that it is enough to take stock of the general will of the constituency as expressed by the majority and that the will of any particular section however much it may be in conflict with the will of the majority may be ignored without remorse and without being guilty of any inequity.

(3) *That* the representative who is elected by the voters will represent the wishes and interests of the voters and that there is not the danger of the representative allowing the interest of his class to dominate and override the interests and wishes of the voter who elects him.

Every one of these assumptions is a false assumption unjustified by any theory and, unsupported by experience. The history of Parliamentary Government furnishes abundant proof in support of this assertion and even the history of England tells the same tale. It is wrong to suppose that the majority in all circumstances can be trusted to represent the will of all sections of people in the constituency. As a matter of fact it can never do so to any satisfactory degree. If at all, it can only give a very pale reflection of the general will and even that capacity for pale reflection must depend upon how numerous and varied are the interests which are consciously -shared by the different sections of the constituency and how full and free is the interplay between than. It is obvious that where, as in India, there are no interest which are shared, where there is no full and free interplay and where there are no common cycles of participation for the different sections, one section large or small cannot represent the will of the other. The will of the majority is the will of the minority and nothing more, and no amount of logical ingenuity can alter the fact and to give effect to it is to allow full play to the tyranny of the Majority.

Again it is wrong to suppose that the representative elected to the Legislature will represent the wishes of the voters who elect him and forget or subordinate the interests of the class to which he belongs. The case of the representative is a case of divided loyalties. He is confronted with two-rather with three- conflicting duties (1) a duty to himself, (2) a duty to the class to which he belongs, and (3) a duty to the voters who have elected him. Omitting (he first from our consideration it is common experience that the representative prefers the interests of his class to that of his voters. And why should any one expect him to *act* otherwise? It is in the nature of things that a man's self should be nearer to him than his constituency. There is a homely saying that man's skin sits closer to him than his shirt. To the members of the Legislature it is true more often than not that his class is his skin and the constituency is a shut which it is unnecessary to say is one degree removed than the skin.

The Hindu therefore in relying upon the territorial constituency is seeking-to base the political structure of India upon foundations which all political architects have declared to be unsound. The territorial constituency has long since been regarded even in European countries as a discredited piece of political mechanism. In great many European countries the representative system based on territorial constituency has been wound up and replaced by other systems of Government largely because the territorial system of representation produced neither good Government nor efficient Government In other countries where representative institutions have survived there is an acute discontent with the result produced by the system of territorial constituencies. The proposals for occupational and functional representation, the proposals for referendum and recall all furnish proof, if proof is really wanted, that there is a great body of enlightened and intelligent opinion which is definitely against the system of territorial constituency.

In these circumstances the question as to why the Hindu insists upon a political mechanism which is discredited everywhere excites a certain amount of curiosity. The reason he gives is that it is the only mechanism which is consistent with nationalism. I am not convinced that this is the real explanation. The real explanation to my mind is very different *The* Hindu prefers the territorial constituency because he knows that it will enable him to collect and concentrate all political power in the hands of the Hindus, and who can deny that his calculation is incorrect ? In a purely territorial constituency the contest, the Hindu knows, will be between a huge majority of Hindu voters and a small minority of Untouchable voters. Given this fact the Hindu majority -if it is a purely territorial constituency - is bound to win in all constituencies. But the Hindus besides relying upon their majority can also rely upon other factors which cannot but work to strengthen that majority. Those factors have their origin in the peculiar nature of the Hindu Society. The Hindu Social system which places communities one above the other is a factor which is bound to have its effect on the result of voting. By the Hindu Social system the Communities are placed in an ascending scale of reverence and a descending scale of contempt. It needs no prophet to predict what effect these social attitudes will have cm voting. No Caste Hindu will cast a vote in favour of an Untouchable candidate, for to him he is too contemptible a person to go to the Legislature. On the other hand there will be found many voters among the Untouchables who would willingly cast their votes for a Hindu candidate in preference to an Untouchable candidate. That is because he is taught to revere the former more than himself or his Untouchable kinsmen. 1 am not mentioning the other means which are often resorted to for catching votes of the poor, illiterate, unconscious, unorganised body of voters which the Untouchables are. A combination of all these circumstances is bound to work in the direction of augmenting the representation of the Hindus-Under a system of purely territorial constituencies it is quite certain the Hindus

in the real sense of the word. The nation does not exist, it is to be created, and I think it will be admitted that the suppression of a distinct and a separate community is not the method of creating a nation. Secondly, it is conceded - as the Hindus have done - that Untouchables should be represented in that Legislature by Untouchable then it cannot be denied that the Untouchable must be a true representative of the Untouchable voters. If this is a correct position then separate electorate is the only mechanism by which real representation can be guaranteed to the Untouchables. The Hindu argument against separate electorate is insubstantial and unsupportable. The premises on which the political demands of the Untouchables are based are admitted by the Hindus. Separate electorate is only a consequence which logically follows from those premises. How can you admit the premise and deny the conclusion? Special electorates are devised as a means of protecting the minorities. Why not permit a minority like the Untouchables to determine what kind of electorate is necessary for its protection? If the Untouchables decide to have separate electorates why should their choice not prevail ? These are questions to which the Hindus can give no answer. The reason is that the real objection to separate electorates by the Hindus is different from this ostensible objection raised in the name of a nation. The real objection is that separate electorate does not permit the Hindus to capture the seats reserved for the Untouchables. On the Other hand the joint electorate does. Let me illustrate the point by a few examples of how joint and separate electorate would work in the constituency. Take the following constituencies from the Madras Presidency.

Name of the Constituency	Total number of Seats for Hindus	Seat reserved for the Untouchables.	Total no of Hindu voters	Total no of Untouchable voters	Ratio of Hindu voters to Untouchable voters
1. Madras City South	2	1	40,626	2,577	16 to 1
2.Chicacole	2	1	83,456	5,125	16 to I
3.Vijayanagram	2	1	47,594	996	49 to 1
4. Amalapuram	1	1	52,805	7,760	7 to 1
5. Ellore	1	1	51,795	5,155	9 to 1
6. Bandar	1	1	84,191	8,723	10 to 1
7. Tenali	2	1	1,32,107	5,732	24 to 1

The figures of the voting strength given in the above table for the seven constituencies taken at random in the Madras Presidency are illuminating. A scrutiny of the above figures is sufficient to show any disinterested person that if there is a separate electorate for the Untouchables in these seven constituencies they would be in a position to elect a man in whom they had complete confidence and who would be independent to fight the battle of the Untouchables on the floor of the Legislature against the representatives of the Hindus. If, on the other hand, there is a joint electorate in these constituencies the representative of the Untouchables would be only a nominal representative *and* not a real representative, for no Untouchable who did not AGree to be a nominee of the Hindus and a tool in their hands could be elected in a joint electorate in which the Untouchable voter was out numbered in ratio of I to 24 or in some cases 1 to 49.. The joint electorate is from the point of the Hindus to use a familiar phrase a "rotten borough" in which the Hindus get the right to nominate an Untouchable to set nominally as a representative of the Untouchables but really as a tool of the Hindus. It will be noticed that the Hindu in opposing the so-called communal Scheme of the Untouchables with his so-called National Scheme is not fighting for a principle nor is be fighting for the nation. He is simply fighting for his own interests. He is fighting to have in his hands the undivided control over political power. His first line of defence is *not* to allow any shares to be drawn up so that like the Manager of the Hindu joint family he can use the whole for his benefit. That is why he fought for purely territorial constituencies. Failing that he takes his second line of defence. He wants that if he is made to concede power he must not lose control over it. This is secured by joint electorates and frustrated by separate electorates. That is why the Hindu objects to separate electorates *and* insists on joint electorates.

The end of the so-called National Scheme may not be communal but the result undoubtedly is.

CHAPTER VI

The Executive

THE SECOND political demand of the Untouchables is that they must not only be represented to the Legislature but they *must* also be represented in the executive. This demand is also opposed by the Hindus. The argument of the Hindus takes two forms. One is that the executive must represent the majority of the Legislature and secondly the men in the Executive must be competent to hold places in the executive. I propose to deal with the second argument first.

It is an argument which is fundamentally sound. But it is equally necessary to realise that in a representative Government this argument cannot be carried too far. For as Professor Dicey has argued, "It has never been a primary object of constitutional arrangement to get together the best possible parliament in intellectual capacity. Indeed, it would be inconsistent with the idea of representative Government to attempt to form a parliament far superior in intelligence to the mass of the nation."

The stress upon competency is needless. Nobody has said that ignorant people should be made Ministers simply because they are Untouchables. Given the right to representation in the cabinet the Untouchables, there is no doubt, will elect the most competent people amongst them- there are a number of than in every province- to fill those places. Again why apply this limiting condition to the Untouchables only ? Like the Untouchables the Muslims are also claiming the right to be represented in the cabinet. Why have the Hindus not insisted upon such a limiting condition against the Muslims' claim?

is open to all castes and creeds will enable the Untouchables to get a footing in the Public Service. That depends upon the educational system of the State. Is it sufficiently democratic? Are the facilities for education sufficiently widespread and sufficiently used to permit persons from all classes to come forth to compete? Otherwise, even with the system of open competition large classes are sure to be left out in the cold. This basic condition is conspicuous by its absence in India. Higher education in India is the monopoly of Hindus and particularly of high Caste Hindus. By reason of Untouchability the Untouchables are denied the opportunity for Education. By reason of their poverty higher education necessary for higher posts in the public service- and higher posts in the public service are the only things that matter because they have a strategic value- is not within their reach. The State will not take the financial responsibility of giving them higher education- they are demanding it by their resolution and the Hindus will not extend the benefit of their charities to the Untouchables- Hindu Charity being shamefully communal- so that to ask the Untouchables to rely upon the results of competitive examination for entry into the public services is to practise a fraud upon than. The position taken up by the Untouchables is in no sense unreasonable. They admit the necessity for maintaining efficiency. That is why in their resolution they themselves say that their demand shall be subject to the rule of minimum qualification. In other words what the Untouchables demand is that a minimum qualification should be prescribed for every post in the public service and if two persons apply for such a post and the Untouchables has the minimum qualification he should be preferred to a Hindu even though the Hindu may have a qualification higher than the minimum qualification. It, of course, does mean that the basis for appointment should be minimum qualification and not the higher qualification. This may sound queer to those who do not mind if their test of efficiency gives certain communities a monopoly of public service. But did not Campbell-Bannerman say that self-government was better than good government? What else are the Untouchables demanding? They are prepared to recognise the need of having an efficient Government. That is why they are ready to accept the requirement of minimum qualifications for entry in the public services of the country. What the untouchables are not prepared to do is to forego self-government for good government Good Government based on highest qualification will be a communal government, for the Hindus alone can claim qualifications higher than minimum qualifications. This is what they do not want. What they say is that minimum qualifications are enough for efficient government and since it makes self-government possible, minimum qualification should be the rule for entry in Public Service. It ensures self-government as well as efficient government.

CHAPTER VIII

Separate Settlements

Resolution No. IV Referred to in the foregoing part of this paper is to my mind quite self-explanatory and not much detailed comment is necessary to explain its purport. Nor is it possible in the compass of this short paper to deal with it in more than general terms. The demand for separate settlements is the result of what might be called "The New Life Movement" among the Untouchables. The object of the movement is to free the Untouchables from the thraldom of the Hindus. So long as the present arrangement continues it is impossible for the Untouchables either to free themselves from the yoke of the Hindus or to get rid of their Untouchability. It is the close-knit association of the Untouchables with the Hindus living in the same villages which marks them out as Untouchables and which enables the Hindus to identify them as being Untouchables. India is admittedly a land of villages and so long as the village system provides an easy method of marking out and identifying the Untouchable, the Untouchable has no escape from Untouchability. It is the village system which perpetuates untouchability and the Untouchables therefore demand that it should be broken and the Untouchables who are as a matter of fact socially separate should be made separate geographically and territorially also, and be grouped into separate villages exclusively of Untouchables in which the distinction of the high and the low and of Touchable and Untouchable will find no place.

The second reason for demanding separate settlements arises out of the economic position of the Untouchables in the village. That their condition is most pitiable no one will deny. They are a body of landless labourers who are entirely dependent upon such employment as the Hindus may choose to give them and on such wages as the Hindus may find it profitable to pay. In the villages in which they live they cannot engage in any trade or occupation, for owing to untouchability no Hindu will deal with them. It is therefore obvious that there is no way of earning a living which is open to the Untouchables so long as they live as a dependent part of the Hindu village. This economic dependence has also other consequences besides the condition of poverty and degradation which proceeds from it. The Hindu has a code of life, which is part of his religion. This code of life gives him many privileges and heaps upon the Untouchable many indignities which are incompatible with the sanctity of human life. By the New Life Movement which has taken hold of the Untouchables, the Untouchables all over India are fighting against the indignities and injustices which the Hindus in the name of their religion have heaped upon them. A perpetual war is going on every day in every village between the Hindus and the Untouchables. It does not see the light of the day. The Hindu Press is not prepared to advertise it lest it should injure the cause of their freedom in the eyes of the world. The silent struggle is however a fact. Under the village system the Untouchable has found himself greatly handicapped in his struggle for free and honourable life. It is a contest between the economically and socially strong Hindus and an economically poor and socially small group of Untouchables. That the Hindus most often succeed in pulling down Untouchables is largely due to many causes. The Hindu has the Police and the Magistracy on his side. In a quarrel between the Untouchables and the Hindus the Untouchables will never get protection from the Police or justice from the Magistrate. The Police and the Magistracy are Hindus, and they love their class more than their duty. But the chief weapon in the armoury of the Hindus is economic power which they possess Over the poor Untouchables living in the village. The economic processes by which the Hindus can hold down the Untouchables in their struggle for equality are well described in the Report made by a Committee appointed by the Government of Bombay in 1928 to investigate into the grievances of the Depressed Classes[2] and from which the following extracts are made. It illuminates the situation in a manner so simple that even foreigners who do not know the mysteries of the Hindu social system may understand what tyranny the Hindus can practise upon the Untouchables. The committee said -

"Although we have recommended various remedies to secure to the Depressed Classes their rights to all public utilities we fear that there will be difficulties in the way of their exercising them for a long time to come. The first difficulty is the fear of open violence against them by the orthodox classes, It must be noted that the Depressed Classes form a small minority in every village, opposed to which is a great majority *of* the orthodox who are bent on protecting their interests and dignity from any supposed invasion by the Depressed Classes at any cost. The danger of prosecution by the Police has put a limitation upon the use of violence by the orthodox classes and consequently such cases axe rare.

"The second difficulty arises from the economic position in which the Depressed Classes are found today. The Depressed Classes have no economic independence in most parts of the Presidency. Some cultivate the lands *of* the orthodox classes as their tenants at will Others live on their earnings as farm labourers employed by the orthodox classes and the rest subsist on the food or grain given to them by the orthodox classes in lieu of service rendered to them as village servants. We have heard of numerous instance where the orthodox classes have used their economic power as a weapon against those Depressed Classes in their villages, when the latter have dared to exercise their rights, and have evicted them from their *land,* and stopped their employment and discontinued their remuneration as village servants. This boycott is often planned on such an extensive scale as to include the prevention of the Depressed Classes from using the commonly used paths and the stoppage of sale of the necessaries of life by the village

---

2. Before The Government of India act 1935 the Untouchables were generally described as the Despressed Classes. The Act calls them Scheduled Castes.

Bania. According to the evidence, sometimes small causes suffice for the proclamation of a social boycott against the Depressed Classes. Frequently it follows on the exercise by the Depressed Classes of their right to the use of the common well, but cases have been *by* no means rare where a stringent boycott has been proclaimed simply because a Depressed Class man has put on the sacred thread, has bought a piece of land, has put on good clothes or ornaments, or has carried a marriage procession with the bride-groom on the horse through the public street."

This demand for separate settlements is a new demand which has been put forth by the Untouchables for the first time. It is not possible to say as yet as to what attitude the Hindus will take to this demand. But there is no doubt that this is the most vital demand made by the Untouchables, and I am sure that whatever may happen with regard to the other demands they are not likely to yield on this. The Hindus are prone to think that they and the Untouchables are joined together by the will of God as the Bible says the husband is joined to his wife and they will say in the language of the Bible that those whom God is pleased to join let no man put asunder. The Untouchables are determined to repudiate any such view of their relations with the Hindus. They want the link to be broken and a complete divorce from the Hindus effected without delay.

The only questions that arise are those of the cost it will involve in and time it will take. As to cost, the Untouchables say it should be financed by Government It will no doubt fall for the most part on the Hindus. But there is no reason why the Hindus should not bear the same. The Hindus own everything. They own the land in this country. They control trade, and they also own the State. Every source of revenue and profit is controlled by them. Other communities and particularly the Untouchables are just hewers of wood and drawers of water. The social system helps the Hindus to have a monopoly of everything. There is no reason why they should not be asked to pay the cost of this scheme when they practically own the country.

As to time, it matters very little even if the transplantation of the Untouchables to new settlements takes 20 years. Those who have been the bounded slaves of the Hindus for a thousand years may well be happy with the prospect of getting their freedom by the end of 20 years.

and reactions, his likes and dislikes. These likes and dislikes, actions and reactions are not institutions which can be lopped off. They are forces and influences which can be dealt with by controlling them or counteracting them. If the social forces are to be prevented from contaminating politics and perverting it to the aggrandisement of the few and the degradation of the many then it follows that the political structure must be so framed that it will contain mechanisms which will bottle the prejudices and nullify the injustice which the social forces are likely to cause if they were let loose.

So far I have explained in a general way why the peculiar social structure of the Hindu Society calls for a peculiar political structure and why the marker of the Indian Constitution cannot escape problems which did not plague the makers of Constitution in other countries. Let me now take the specific question, namely why it is necessary that in the Indian Constitution the Communal Scheme must find its place and why in the Public Services for the Untouchables should be specified and should be assigned to them as their separate possession. The justification for these demands is easy and obvious. It arises from the undeniable fact that what divides the Untouchables from the Hindus is not mere matter of difference on non-essentials. It is a case of fundamental antagonism and antipathy. No evidence of this antipathy and antagonism is necessary. The system of Untouchability is enough evidence of the inherent antagonism between the Hindus and the Untouchables. Given this antagonism it is simply impossible to ask the Untouchables to depend upon and trust the Hindus to do them justice when the Hindu get their freedom and independence from the British. Who can say that the Untouchable is not right in saying that he will not trust the Hindu ? The Hindu is as alien to him as a European is and what is worse the European alien is neutral but the Hindu is most shamefully partial to his own class and antagonistic to the Untouchables. There can be no doubt that the Hindus have all these ages despised, disregarded and disowned the Untouchables as belonging to a different and contemptible strata of Society if not to a different race. By their own code of conduct the Hindus behave as the most exclusive class steeped in their own prejudices and never sharing the aspirations of the Untouchables with whom they have nothing to do and whose interests are opposed to theirs. Why should the Untouchables entrust their fate to such people ? How could the Untouchables be legitimately asked to leave their interest into the hands of a people who as a matter of fact are opposed to them in their motives and interests, who do not sympathise with the living forces operating among the Untouchables, who are themselves not charged with their wants, cravings and desires, who are inimical to their aspirations, who in all certainty will deny justice to them and to discriminate against them and who by reason of the sanction of their religion have not been and will not be ashamed to practise against the Untouchables any kind of inhumanity. The only safety against such people is to have the political rights which the Untouchables claim as safeguards against the tyranny of the Hindu Majority defined in the Constitution. Are the Untouchables extravagant in demanding this safety ?

CHAPTER X

Some Questions to the Hindus and their Friends

In the midst of this political controversy one notices that the Hindus are behaving differently towards different communities. The Untouchables are not the only people in India who are demanding political safeguards. Like the Untouchables the Muslims and the Sikhs have also presented their political demands to the Hindus. Both the Mussulmans and the Sikhs can in no sense be called helpless minorities. On the contrary they are the two most powerful communities in India. They are educationally quite advanced and economically well placed. By their social standing they are quite as high as the Hindus. Their organisation is a solid structure and no Hindu will dare to take any liberties with them much less cause any harm to them.

What are the political demands of the Muslims and the Sikhs? It is not possible to set them out here. But the general opinion is that they are very extravagant and the Hindus resent them very much. In contrast with this the condition and the demands of the Untouchables are just the opposite of the condition of the Muslims and the Sikhs. They are a weak, helpless and despised minority. They are at the mercy of all and there are not a few occasions when Hindus, Muslims and Sikhs combine to oppress them. Of all the Minorities they need the greatest protection and the strongest safeguards. Their demands are of the modest kind and there is nothing in them of that over-insurance which may be said to characterise the demands of the Muslims and the Sikhs. What is the reaction of the Hindus to the demands of the Muslims, the Sikhs and the Untouchables? Notwithstanding the extravagance of their demands the Hindus are ever ready to conciliate the Mussalmans and the Sikhs, particularly the former. They not only want to be correct in their relationship with the Mussalmans, they are prepared to be considerate and even generous. Mr. Rajagopalachari's political exploits are too fresh to be forgotten. Suddenly he enrolled himself as a soldier of the Muslim League and proclaimed a war on his own kin and former

friends and for what ? Not for their not failure to grant the reasonable demands of the Muslim but for their conceding the most extravagant one, namely Pakistan !! What is Mr. Rajagopalachari's response to the demands of the Untouchables ? So far I am aware there is no response. He does not even seem to be aware that there are 60 million Untouchables in this country and that they too like the Muslims are demanding political safeguards. This attitude of studied silence and cold indifference of Mr. Rajagopalachari is typical of the whole body of Hindus. The Hindus have been opposing the political demands of the Untouchables with the tenacity of. a bulldog and the perversity of a renegade. The Press is theirs and they make a systematic attempt to ignore the Untouchables. When they fail to ignore them they buy their leaders; and where they find a leader not open to purchase they systematically abuse him, misrepresent him, blackmail him, and do everything possible that lies in their power to suppress him and silence him: Any such leader who is determined to fight for the cause of the Untouchables he and his followers are condemned as anti-National. So exasperated the Hindus become by the political demands of the Untouchables that they in their rage refuse to recognise how generous the Untouchables are in consenting to be ruled by a Hindu Majority in return for nothing more than a few political safeguards. *The* Hindus are not aware of what Carson said to Redmond when the two were negotiating for a United Ireland. The incident is worth recalling. Redmond said to Carson "Ask any safeguards you like for the Protestant Minority of Ulster, I am prepared to give them; but let us have a United Ireland under one constitution." Carson's reply was curt and brutal. He said without asking for time to consider the offer "Damn your safeguards, I don't want to be ruled by you". The Hindus ought to be thankful that the Untouchables have not taken the attitude which Carson took. But far from being thankful they are angry because the Untouchables are daring to ask for political rights. In the opinion of the Hindus the Untouchables have no right to ask for any rights. What does this difference of attitude on the part of the Hindus to the political demands of the different communities indicate? It indicates three things (1) They want to *get* all power to themselves, (2) They are not prepared to base their political institutions on the principle of justice, (3) Where they have to surrender power they will surrender it to the forces of truculence and the mailed first but never to the dictates of justice.

This attitude of the Hindus forms the tragic scene of Indian politics. Unfortunately this is not the only tragic scene with Indian Politics. There is another equally tragic in character. It concerns the friends of the Hindus in foreign countries, The Hindus have created many friends for themselves all over the world by their clever propaganda, particularly in America, "the land of liberty". *The* tragedy is that these friends of the Hindus are supporting a side without examining whether it is the side which they in point of justice ought to support No American friends of the Hindus have, so far as I know, asked what do the Hindus stand for ? Are they fighting for freedom or are they fighting for power ? If the Hindus are fighting for power, are the American friends justified in helping the Hindus ? If the Hindus are engaged in a war *for* freedom, must they not be asked to declare their war aims? This is the least bit these American friends could do. Since the American friends have thought it fit to respond to the Hindu call for help it is necessary to tell these American friends of the Hindus what wrong they will be doing to the cause of freedom by their indiscriminate and blind support to the Hindu side. What I want to say follows the line of argument which the Hindus themselves have taken. Since the war started the Hindus, both inside and outside the *Congress,* demanded that the British should declare their *war* aims. Day in and day out the British were told, " If you want our help, tell us what you are fighting for? If you are fighting for freedom, tell us if you will give us. freedom in the name of which you are waging this war" There was a stage when the Hindus were prepared to be satisfied with a promise from the British that India will have the benefit of freedom for which the British are waging. They have gone a stage further. They are no longer content with a promise. Or to put it in the language of a Congressman, "They refuse to accept a post-dated cheque on a crashing Bank". They wanted freedom to be given right now, before the Hindus would consent to give their voluntary support to the War effort. That is the significance of Mr. Gandhi's new slogan of "Quit India". Mr. Churchill on whom the responsibility of answering these questions fell replied, that his war aim was victory over the enemy. The Hindus were not satisfied. They questioned him further "What are you going to do after you get that victory ? What social order you propose to establish after the war ?" There was a storm when Mr. Churchil replied that he hoped to restore traditional Britain. These were legitimate   questions I agree. But do not the friends of Hindus think that if it is legitimate to ask the very same questions to Mr. Churchill it is also legitimate to ask the very same questions to Mr. Gandhi and-the Hindus ? The British had declared war against Hitler. Mr. Gandhi has declared war against the British. The British have an Empire. So have the Hindus. For is not Hinduism a form of I imperialism and are not the Untouchables a subject race, owing there allegiance and their servitude to their Hindu Master ? If Churchill must be asked to declare his war aims how could anybody avoid asking Mr. Gandhi and the Hindus to declare their war aims 7 Both say their war is a war for freedom. If that is so both have a duty to declare what their war aims are. What does Mr. Gandhi propose to do after he gets his victory over the British 7 Does he propose to use the freedom he hopes to get to make the Untouchables free or will he allow the freedom he gets to be used to endow the Hindus with more power than they now possess, to hold the Untouchables as their bondsmen ? Will

Mr. Gandhi arid Hindus establish a New Older or will they be content with rehabilitation of the traditional Hindu India, with its castes and its untouchability, with its denial of Liberty, Equality and Fraternity 71 should think that these questions should be asked by those American friends to Mr. Gandhi and the Hindus who are helping them in this so-called war for Freedom. These questions are legitimate and pertinent. It is only answers to such questions which will enable these American friends to know whether Mr. Gandhi's war is a war for freedom or a war for power. These questions are not merely pertinent and legitimate, they are also necessary. The reason is obvious to those who know the Hindus. The Hindus have an innate and inveterate conservatism and they have a religion which is incompatible with liberty, equality and fratemity i. e. with democracy. Inequality, no doubt, exists everywhere in the world. It is largely to conditions and circumstances. But it never has had the support of religion. With the Hindus it is different. There is not only inequality in Hindu Society but inequality is the official doctrine of the Hindu religion. The Hindu has no will to equality. His inclination and his attitude are opposed to the democratic doctrine of one man one value. Every Hindu is a social Tory and political Radical. Mr Gandhi is no exception to this rule. He presents himself to the world as a liberal but his liberalism is only a very thin veneer which sits very lightly on him as dust does on one's boots. You scratch him and you will find that underneath his liberalism he is a blue blooded Tory. He stands for the cursed caste. He is a fanatic Hindu upholding the Hindu religion. See how the Hindus read the famous American Declaration of Independence of 1776. The Hindu is mad with joy when he reads the Declaration to say-

That whenever any Form of Government become destructive of these ends, it is the Right of the People to alter or to abolish it, and to institute new Government, laying its foundation on such principles and organising its powers in such form, as to them shall seem most likely to effect their Safety and Happiness.'

But he stops there. He never bothers about the earlier part of that Declaration which says :-

"We hold these truths to be self-evident, that all men are created equal, that they are endowed by their Creator with certain unalienable Rights, that among these are Life, Liberty and the pursuit of Happiness. That to secure these rights. Governments are instituted among Men, deriving their just powers from the consent of the governed."

The implementation of this Declaration has no doubt been a tragic episode in the history of the United States. There have been two views about this document Some hold that it is a great spiritual document. Others have held that it immoralises many untruths. In any case this charter of human Liberty was not applied to the Negroes. What is however important to note is the faith underlying the Declaration. There is no doubt about it and certainly no doubt about the faith of Jefferson, the author of this Declaration. He never forgot that while enunciating along principle, his country decided to take a short step. He wrote, "I am sorry for my countrymen." It may be no. recompense to the Negroes. But it is by no means small comfort to know that the conscience of the country is not altogether dead and the flame of righteous indignation may one day bust forth. The Negroes may laugh at this. But the fact is that even this much comfort the Untouchables cannot hope to have from the Hindus. People today are proud of the fact that the Hindus are a solid mass. But strange as it may appear, to the Untouchables of India, this is more a matter of dread than comfort-as the "Solid South" is to the Negroes in the United States. Where could anyone find in India among the Hindus any person with a sense of shame and a sense of remorse such as was felt by Jefferson ? I should have thought the Hindus would be too ashamed of this stigma of Untouchability on them to appear before the world with a demand for their freedom. That they do clamour for freedom- the pity is that they get support- is evidence that their conscience is dead, that they feel no righteous indignation, and to them Untouchability is neither a moral sit) nor a civil wrong. It is just a sport as cricket or hockey is. The friends of Mr. Gandhi will no doubt point to him and his work. But what has Mr. Gandhi done to reform Hindu Society that his work and life be cited by democrats

as a witness of hope and assurance 7 His friends have been informed of the Harijan Sevak Sangh and they continue to ask, "Is not Mr. Gandhi working to uplift the Harijans ?" Is he ? What is the object of this Hanjan Sevak Sangh ? Is it to prepare the Untouchables to win their freedom from their Hindu masters, to make them their social and political equals ? Mr. Gandhi had never had any such object before him and he never wants to do this, and I say that he cannot do this. This is the task of a democrat and a revolutionary. Mr. Gandhi is neither. He is a Tory by birth as well as by faith. The work of the Harijan Sevak Sangh is not to raise the Untouchables. His main object, as every self-respecting Untouchable knows, is to make India safe for Hindus and Hinduism. He is certainly not fighting the battle of the Untouchables. On the contrary by distributing through the Harijan Sevak Sangh petty gifts to petty Untouchables he is buying, benumbing and drawing the laws of the opposition of the Untouchables which he knows is the only force which will disrupt the caste system and will establish real democracy in India. Mr. Gandhi wants Hinduism and the Hindu caste system to remain intact. Mr. Gandhi also wants the Untouchables to remain as Hindus. But as what 7 not as partners but as poor relations of the Hindus. Mr. Gandhi is kind to the Untouchables. But for what ? Only because he wants to kill, by kindness, them and their movement for separation and independence from Hindus. The Harijan Sevak Sangh is one of the many techniques which has enabled Mr. Gandhi to be a successful humbug.

Turn to Pandit Jawaharlal Nehru. He draws his inspiration from the Jeffersonian Declaration; but has he ever expressed any shame or any remorse about the condition of the 60 millions of Untouchables ? Has he anywhere referred to them in the torrent of literature which comes out from his pen ? Go to the youth of India, if you want. The youths who fill the Universities and who follow the Pandit's lead are ever ready to fight the political battle of India against the British. But what do these children of the leisured class Hindus have done to redress the wrongs their forefathers have done to the Untouchables ? You can get thousands of Hindu youths to join political propaganda but you cannot get one single youth to take up the cause of breaking the caste system or of removing Untouchability. Democracy and democratic life, justice and conscience which are sustained by a belief in democratic principle are foreign to the Hindu mind. To leave democracy and freedom in such Tory hands would be the greatest mistake democrats could commit It is therefore very necessary for the American friends of the Hindus to ask Mr. Gandhi and the Hindus to declare their War aims, so that they may be sure that the fight of the Hindus against British is really and truly a fight for freedom. The Congress and the Hindus will no doubt refer their inquiring foreign friends to the Congress Resolutions regarding minority rights. But I would like to warn the American friends of the Hindus not to be content with the "glittering generalities" contained in congress declaration of Minority Rights. To declare the rights of the minority is one thing and to have them implemented is another. And why should the friends of the Hindus if they are really friends of freedom, not insist on implementation straight away? Are not the Hindus saying that they would not be satisfied with mere declaration of freedom from the British ? Are they not asking for immediate implementation ? If they want the British to implement their War aims, why should the Hindus be not prepared to implement their war aims ? American friends of the Hindus, I am sure, will not be misled by the Hindu propaganda that this war of the Hindus against the British is a War for freedom. Before helping the Hindus they must get themselves satisfied that the Hindus who are urging that their war against the British is a war for freedom will not turn out to be the enemies of the freedom of millions of Indians like the Untouchables. That is the plea I am making on behalf of the 60 millions of the Untouchables of India. And above all let not the American friends think that checks and balances in a Constitution-the demand for checks and balances suited to Indian conditions-are not necessary because the struggle is carried on by a people and is carried on in the name of freedom. Friends of democracy and freedom cannot afford to forget the words of John Adams when he said-

"We may appeal to every page of history we have hitherto turned over, for proof irrefragable that the people when they have been unchecked, have been as unjust, tyrannical, brutal, barbarous , and cruel as any king or Senate possessed of uncontrollable power : the majority has eternally and without one exception usurped over the rights of the minority."

If all Majorities must be subjected to checks and balances how much more must it be so in the case of the Hindus ?